# YOU, EMPERORS, AND OTHERS: Poems 1957-1960

BOOKS BY ROBERT PENN WARREN

John Brown: The Making of a Martyr
Thirty-six Poems
Night Rider
Eleven Poems on the Same Theme
At Heaven's Gate
Selected Poems, 1923-1943
All the King's Men
The Circus in the Attic
World Enough and Time
Brother to Dragons
Band of Angels
Segregation: The Inner Conflict in the South
Promises: Poems 1954-1956
Selected Essays
The Cave
You, Emperors, and Others: Poems 1957-1960

# YOU, EMPERORS, AND OTHERS

## Poems 1957-1960

ROBERT PENN WARREN

RANDOM HOUSE NEW YORK

First Printing

 Published in New York by Random House, Inc., and simultaneously in Toronto, Canada, by Random House of Canada, Limited.

Library of Congress Catalog Card Number: 60-12123

Manufactured in the United States of America

These poems have appeared in the *Partisan Review, Yale Review, American Scholar, Saturday Review, Kenyon Review, Virginia Quarterly Review, Prairie Schooner, Sewanee Review, Delta, and Botteghe Oscure.*

*To Max and Carol Shulman*

## *Contents*

### *Garland for You*



### *Two Pieces after Suetonius*



### *Mortmain*

## *Prognosis: A Short Story, the End of Which You Will Know Soon Enough*



## *Autumnal Equinox on Mediterranean Beach* 

## *Nursery Rhymes*



## *Short Thoughts for Long Nights*

***YOU, EMPERORS, AND OTHERS: Poems 1957-1960***

## ***Garland for You***

### 1 CLEARLY ABOUT YOU

*Bene fac, hoc tecum feres.*

—On tomb of Roman citizen of no historical importance, under the Empire

Whoever you are, this poem is clearly about you,
For there's nothing else in the world it could be about.
Whatever it says, this poem is clearly true,
For truth is all we are born to, and the truth's out.

You won't look in the mirror? Well—but your face is there
Like a face drowned deep under water, mouth askew,
And tongue in that mouth tastes cold water, not sweet air,
And if it could scream in that medium, the scream would be you.

Your mother preferred the more baroque positions.
Your father's legerdemain marks the vestry accounts.
So you didn't know? Well, it's time you did—though one shuns
To acknowledge the root from which one's own virtue mounts.

In the age of denture and reduced alcoholic intake,
When the crow's dawn-calling stirs memory you'd better eschew,
You will try the cross, or the couch, for balm for the heart's ache—
But that stranger who's staring so strangely, he knows you are you.

Things are getting somewhat out of hand now—light fails on the marshes.
In the back lot the soft-faced delinquents are whistling like snipe.
The apples you stored in the cellar are acerb and harsh as
The heart that on bough of the bosom all night will not ripe.

Burn this poem, though it wring its small hands and cry *alack.*
But no use, for in bed, into your pajama pocket,
It will creep, and sleep as snug as a field mouse in haystack,
And its heart to your heart all night make a feather-soft racket.

## 2 LULLABY: EXERCISE IN HUMAN CHARITY AND SELF-KNOWLEDGE

*Mr. and Mrs. North and South America, and all the ships at sea, let's go to press.*
—Greeting of radio broadcast by Walter Winchell

Sleep, my dear, whatever your name is:
Galactic milk spills down light years.
Sleep, my dear, your personal fame is
Sung safely now by all the tunèd spheres,
And your sweet identity
Fills like vapor, pale in moonlight, all the infinite night sky.
You are you, and naught's to fear:
Sleep, my dear.

Sleep, my dear, whatever your face is,
Fair or brown, or young or old.
Sleep, my dear, your airs and graces
Are the inner logic History will unfold,
And what faults you suffer from
Will refract, sand grain in sun-glare, glory of that light to come.
You are you, all will be clear;
So sleep, my dear.

Sleep, my dear, whatever your sex is,
Male or female, bold or shy.
What need now for that sweet nexus
In dark with some strange body you lie by?
What need now to seek that contact

That shows self to itself as merely midnight's dearest artifact?
For you to yourself, at last, appear
Clearly, my dear.

But are you she, pale hair wind-swept,
Whose face night-glistened in sea fog?
Or she, pronouncing joy, who wept
In that desperate noontide by the cranberry bog?
Or only that face in the crowd, caught
And borne like a leaf on the flood away, to which I gave one perturbed thought?
Yes, which are you? Yes, turn your face here
As you sleep, dear.

No, no, dearest, none of these—
For I who bless can bless you only
For the fact our histories
Can have no common bond except the lonely
Fact of humanness we share
As now, in place and fate disparate, we breathe the same dark pulsing air.
Where you lie now, far or near,
Sleep, my dear.

Sleep, my dear, wherever now
Your shadowy head finds place to rest.
Stone or bosom, bed or hedgerow—
All the same, and all the same are blest
If, receiving that good freight,
They sustain it, uncomplaining, till cock-crow makes the dark abate.
Whoever I am, what I now bless
Is your namelessness.

## 3 MAN IN THE STREET

*Raise the stone, and there thou shalt find Me, cleave the wood, there am I.*
*—The Sayings of Jesus*

"Why are your eyes as big as saucers—big as saucers?"
I said to the man in the gray flannel suit.
And he said: "I see facts I can't refute—
Winners and losers,
Pickers and choosers,
Takers, refusers,
Users, abusers,
And my poor head, it spins like a top.
It spins and spins, and will not stop."
Thus said the young man I happened to meet,
Wearing his nice new Ivy League flannel suit down the sunlit street.

"What makes you shake like wind in the willows—wind in the willows?"
I said to the man in the black knit tie.
And he said: "I see things before my eye—
Jolly good fellows,
Glad-handers of hellos,
Fat windbags and bellows,
Plumpers of pillows,
And God's sweet air is like dust on my tongue,
And a man can't stand such things very long."
Thus said the young man I happened to meet,
Wearing his gray flannel suit and black knit tie down the sunlit street.

"What makes your face flour-white as a miller's—white as a miller's?"
I said to the man in the Brooks Brothers shirt.
And he said: "I see things that can't help but hurt—
Backers and fillers,
Pickers and stealers,
Healers and killers,
Ticklers and feelers,
And I go to prepare a place for you,
For this location will never do."
Said the nice young man I happened to meet,
Wearing gray flannel suit, knit tie, and Brooks Brothers shirt down the sunlit street.

## 4 SWITZERLAND

*. . . world-mecca for seekers of pleasure and health . . .*

—Travel agency brochure

After lunch take the half-destroyed bodies and put them to bed.
For a time a mind's active behind the green gloom of the jalousie,
But soon each retires inside the appropriate head
To fondle, like childhood's stuffed bear, the favorite fallacy.

In their pairings the young, of course, have long since withdrawn,
But they take more time to come to the point of siesta:
There's the beach-fatigue and the first digestion to wait on,
So it's three by the time one's adjusted one's darling, and pressed her.

Here are many old friends you have known from long, long back,
Though of course under different names and with different faces.
Yes, they are the kind of whom you never lose track,
And there's little difference, one finds, between different places.

That's why travel is broadening—you can, for example, expect
The aging alcoholic you once knew in San Diego.
Or the lady theologian who in bed likes best her own intellect:
Lady Hulda House, *Cantab.*—for therapy now trying a dago.

There's the sweet young divorcée whose teacher once said she should write.
There's the athlete who stares at himself in the glass, by the hour.
There's the old man who can't forgive, and wakes in the night:
*Forgive—forgive what?* To remember is beyond his power.

And the others and all, they all here re-enact
The acts you'd so shrewdly remarked at the very start,
When in other resorts you first met them—many, in fact,
In that high, highly advertised Switzerland of your own heart.

O God of the *steinbock's* great sun-leap—Ice-spike in ice-chasm—
Let down Thy strong hand to all whom their fevers destroy
And past all their pain, need, greed, lip-biting, and spasm,
Deliver them all, young and old, to Thy health, named joy.

## 5 A REAL QUESTION CALLING FOR SOLUTION

*There is however one peculiar inconsistency which we may note as marking this and many other psychological theories. They place the soul in the body and attach it to the body without trying in addition to determine the reason why or the condition of the body under which such attachment is produced. This would seem however to be a real question calling for solution.*

—Aristotle: *Psychology* 3, 22-23

Don't bother a bit, you are only a dream you are having,
And if when you wake your symptoms are not relieved,
That is only because you harbor a morbid craving
For belief in the old delusion in which you have always believed.

Yes, there was the year when every morning you ran
A mile before breakfast—yes, and the year you read
Virgil two hours just after lunch and began
Your practice of moral assessment, before the toothbrush and bed.

But love boiled down like porridge in a pot,
And beyond the far snow-fields westward, redder than hate,
The sun burned; and one night much better forgot,
Pity, like sputum, gleamed on the station floor-boards, train late.

When you slept on a board you found your back much better.
When you took the mud baths you found that verse came easy.
When you slept with another woman you found that the letter
You owed your wife was a pleasure to write, gay now and teasy.

There once was a time when you thought you would understand
Many things, many things, including yourself, and learn Greek,
But light changes old landscape, and your own hand
Makes signs unseen in the dark, and lips move but do not speak,

For given that vulture and vector which is the stroke
Of the clock absolute on the bias of midnight, memory
Is nothing, is nothing, not even the memory of smoke
Dispersed on windless ease in the great fuddled head of the sky,

And all recollections are false, and all you suffer
Is only the punishment thought appropriate for guilt
You never had, but wish you had the crime for,
For the bitterest tears are those shed for milk—or blood—not spilt.

There is only one way, then, to make things hang together,
Which is to accept the logic of dream, and avoid
Night air, politics, French sauces, autumn weather,
And the thought that, on your awaking, identity may be destroyed.

## 6 THE LETTER ABOUT MONEY, LOVE, OR OTHER COMFORT, IF ANY

*In the beginning was the Word.*
—The Gospel according to St. John

Having accepted the trust so many years back,
before seven wars, nine coups d'état, and the deaths of friends and friendships,
before having entered the world of lurkers, shirkers, burkers, tipsters and tips,
or even discovered I had small knack
for honesty, but only a passion, like a disease, for Truth,
having, as I have said, accepted the trust
those long years back in my youth,
it's no wonder that now I admit, as I must,
to no recollection whatever
of wens, moles, scars, or his marks of identification—but do recall my disgust
at odor of garlic and a somewhat perfervid eye-gleam beneath the dark hat
of the giver,

Who, as I came up the walk in summer moonlight
and set first foot to the porch step, rose with a cough from beside the hydrangea,
and thrust the thing out at me, as though it were common for any total stranger
to squat by one's door with a letter at night,
at which, in surprise, I had stopped to stare (the address even then but a smudge)
until at the burst of his laugh, like a mirthful catarrh,
I turned, but before I could budge
saw the pattering *V*'s of his shoe tips mar
the moon-snowy dew of the yard,
and be gone—an immigrant type of pointed toe and sleazy insouciance
more natural by far
to some Mediterranean alley or merd-spangled *banlieue* than to any boulevard,

Or surely to Dadston, Tenn., and so I was stuck,
for though my first thought was to drop the thing in the mail
and forget the affair,
on second glance I saw what at first I had missed, as though the words
hadn't been there:
*By Hand Only*, and I was dumb-cluck
enough to drive over to Nashville next day to find the address, but found
you had blown, the rent in arrears, your bathroom a sty,
and thus the metaphysical runaround
which my life became, and for which I
have mortgaged all, began,
and I have found milk rotting in bottles inside the back door,
and newspapers knee-high
the carrier had left and never got paid for, and once at a question
a child up and ran

Screaming like bloody murder to fall out of breath,
and once in Dubuque you had sold real estate, and left with a church letter,
Episcopal, High, and at the delicious New England farmhouse
your Llewellin setter
was found in the woodshed, starved to death,
and in Via Margutta you made the attempt, but someone smelled gas at the door
in the nick of time, and you fooled with the female Fulbrights
at the Deux Magots and the Flore,
until the police caught you dead to rights—
oh, it's all so human and sad,
for money and love are terrible things with which to fill
all our human days and nights,
and nobody blames you much, not even I, despite all the trouble I've had,

And still have, on your account, and if it were not
for encroaching age, new illness, and recurring effects of the beating
I took from those hoods in the bar in Frisco for the mere fact
of merely repeating
that financial gossip, and from which I got
this bum gam, my defect in memory, and a slight stutter—
but as I was saying, were it not for my infirm years,
I would try to deliver the letter,
especially since I was moved nigh to tears
myself by the tale you'd been caught
crouched in the dark in the canna bed that pretties the lawn
of the orphanage where it appears
you were raised—yes, crooning among the ruined lilies to a teddy bear,
not what a grown man ought

To be doing past midnight, but be that as it may,
there's little choice for my future course, given present circumstances,
and my conscience is clear, for I assure you I've not made a penny,
at least not expenses,
and so on the basis of peasant hearsay,
at the goatherd's below timber line, I will go up, and beyond the north face,
find that shelf where a last glacial kettle, beck, or cirque glints
blue steel to sky in that moon-place,
and there, while hands bleed and breath stints,
will, on a flat boulder not
far from the spot where you at night drink, leave the letter,
and my obligation to all intents,
weighted by stones like a cairn, with a red bandanna to catch your eye, but what

Good any word of money or love or more casual
comfort may do now, God only knows, for one who by dog and gun
has been hunted to the upper altitudes, for the time comes when all men will shun
you, and you, like an animal,
will crouch among the black boulders and whine under knife edge of night-blast,
waiting for hunger to drive you down to forage
for bark, berries, mast,
roots, rodents, grubs, and such garbage,
or a sheep like the one you with teeth killed,
for you are said to be capable now of all bestiality, and only your age
makes you less dangerous; so, though I've never seen your face and have fulfilled

The trust, discretion, as well as perhaps a strange shame,
overcomes curiosity, and past that high rubble of the world's wrack,
will send me down through darkness of trees until, having lost all track,
I stand, bewildered, breath-bated and lame,
at the edge of a clearing, to hear, as first birds stir, life lift now night's hasp,
then see, in first dawn's drench and drama, the snow peak go gory,
and the eagle will unlatch crag-clasp,
fall, and at breaking of wing-furl, bark glory,
and by that new light I shall seek
the way, and my peace with God, and if in some taproom travelers pry
into this story,
I shall not reduce it to drunken marvel, assuming I know the tongue they speak.

## 7 ARROGANT LAW

*This inner life may be compared to the unrolling of a coil . . .*
—Henri Bergson: *An Introduction to Metaphysics*

Have you crouched with rifle, in woods, in autumn,
In earshot of water where at dawn deer come,
Through gold leafage drifting, through dawn-mist like mist,
And the blue steel sweats cold in your fist?
Have you stood on the gunwale and eyed blaze of sky,
Then with blaze blazing black in your inner eye,
Plunged—plunged to break the anchor's deep hold
On rock, where undercurrents thrill cold?
*Time unwinds like a falling spool.*

Have you lain by your love, at night, by willows,
And heard the stream stumble, moon-drunk, at its shallows,
And heard the cows stir, sigh, and shift space,
Then seen how moonlight lay on the girl's face,
With her eyes hieratically closed, and your heart bulged
With what abrupt Truth to be divulged—
But desolate, desolate, turned from your love,
Knowing you'd never know what she then thought of?
*Time unwinds like a falling spool.*

Have you stood beside your father's bed
While life retired from the knowledgeable head
To hole in some colding last lurking-place,
And standing there studied that strange face,
Which had endured thunder and even the tears

Of mercy in its human years,
But now, past such accident, seemed to withdraw
Into more arrogant dispensation, and law?
*Time unwinds like a falling spool.*

## 8 THE SELF THAT STARES

*John Henry said to the Captain, "A man ain't nothing but a man."*

A folk ballad

Have you seen that brute trapped in your eye
When he realizes that he, too, will die?
Stare into the mirror, stare
At his dawning awareness there.
If man, put razor down, and stare.
If woman, stop lipstick in mid-air.
Yes, pity makes that gleam you gaze through—
Or is that brute now pitying you?
Time unwinds like a falling spool.
We have learned little in that school.

No, nothing, nothing, is ever learned
Till school is out and the books are burned,
And then the lesson will be so sweet
All you will long for will be to repeat
All the sad, exciting process
By which ignorance grew less
In all that error and gorgeous pain
That you may not live again.
What is that lesson? To recognize
The human self naked in your own eyes.

## *Two Pieces after Suetonius*

### 1 APOLOGY FOR DOMITIAN

He was not bad, as emperors go, not really—
Not like Tiberius cruel, or poor Nero silly.
The trouble was only that omens said he would die,
So what could he, mortal, do? Not worse, however, than you might, or I.

Suppose from long back you had known the very hour—
"Fear the fifth hour"—and yet for all your power
Couldn't strike it out from the day, or the day from the year,
Then wouldn't you have to strike something at least? If you did,
would it seem so queer?

Suppose you were proud of your beauty, but baldness set in?
Suppose your good leg were dwindling to spindly and thin?
Wouldn't you, like Domitian, try the classic bed-stunt
To prove immortality on what was propped to bear the imperial brunt?

Suppose you had dreamed a gold hump sprouted out of your back,
And such prosperous burden oppressed you to breath-lack;
Suppose lightning scorched the sheets in your own bedroom;
And from your own statue storm yanked the name plate and chucked it into a tomb—

Well, it happened to him. Therefore, there's little surprise
That for hours he'd lock himself up to pull wings from flies.

Fly or man, what odds? He would wander his hall of moonstone,
Mirror-bright so he needn't look over his shoulder to know that he was alone.

Let's stop horsing around—it's not Domitian, it's you
We mean, and the omens are bad, very bad, and it's true
That virtue comes hard in face of the assigned clock,
And music, at sunset, faint as a dream, is heard from beyond the burdock,

And as for Domitian, the first wound finds the groin,
And he claws like a cat, but the blade continues to go in,
And the body is huddled forth meanly, and what ritual
It gets is at night, and from his old nurse, a woman poor, nonpolitical.

## 2 TIBERIUS ON CAPRI

(a)

*All is nothing, nothing all:*
To tired Tiberius soft sang the sea thus,
Under his cliff-palace wall.
The sea, in soft approach and repulse,
Sings thus, and Tiberius,
Sea-sad, stares past the dusking sea-pulse
Yonder, where come,
One now by one, the lights, far off, of Surrentum.
He stares in the blue dusk-fall,
For all is nothing, nothing all.

Let darkness up from Asia tower.
On that darkening island behind him *spintriae* now stir.
In grot and scented bower,
They titter, yawn, paint lip, grease thigh,
And debate what role each would prefer
When they project for the Emperor's eye
Their expertise
Of his Eastern lusts and complex Egyptian fantasies.
But darkward he stares in that hour,
Blank now in totality of power.

(b)

There once, on that goat island, I,
As dark fell, stood and stared where Europe stank.
Many were soon to die—
From acedia snatched, from depravity, virtue,
Or frolic, not knowing the reason, in rank
On rank hurled, or in bed, or in church, or
Dishing up supper,
Or in a dark doorway, loosening the girl's elastic to tup her,
While high in the night sky,
The murderous tear dropped from God's eye;

And faintly forefeeling, forefearing, all
That to fulfill our time, and heart, would come,
I stood on the crumbling wall
Of that foul place, and my lungs drew in
Scent of dry gorse on the night air of autumn,
And I seized, in dark, a small stone from that ruin,
And I made outcry
At the paradox of powers that would grind us like grain, small and dry.
Dark down, the stone, in its fall,
Found the sea: I could do that much, after all.

## *Mortmain*

### 1 AFTER NIGHT FLIGHT SON REACHES BEDSIDE OF ALREADY UNCONSCIOUS FATHER, WHOSE RIGHT HAND LIFTS IN A SPASMODIC GESTURE, AS THOUGH TRYING TO MAKE CONTACT: 1955

In Time's concatenation and
Carnal conventicle, I,
Arriving, being flung through dark and
The abstract flight-grid of sky,
Saw rising from the sweated sheet and
Ruck of bedclothes ritualistically
Reordered by the paid hand
Of mercy—saw rising the hand—

Christ, start again! What was it I,
Standing there, travel-shaken, saw
Rising? What could it be that I,
Caught sudden in gut- or conscience-gnaw,
Saw rising out of the past, which I
Saw now as twisted bedclothes? Like law,
The hand rose cold from History
To claw at a star in the black sky,

But could not reach that far—oh, cannot!
And the star horribly burned, burns,
For in darkness the wax-white clutch could not
Reach it, and white hand on wrist-stem turns,
Lifts in last tension of tendon, but cannot

Make contact—*oh, oop-si-daisy,* churns
The sad heart, *oh, atta-boy, daddio's got*
*One more shot in the locker, peas-porridge hot—*

But no. Like an eyelid the hand sank, strove
Downward, and in that darkening roar,
All things—all joy and the hope that strove,
The failed exam, the admired endeavor,
Prizes and prinkings, and the truth that strove,
And back of the Capitol, boyhood's first whore—
Were snatched from me, and I could not move,
Naked in that black blast of his love.

## 2 A DEAD LANGUAGE: CIRCA 1885

Father dead, land lost, stepmother haggard with kids,
Big Brother skedaddling off to Mexico
To make his fortune, gold or cattle or cards,
What could he do but what we see him doing?
Cutting crossties for the first railroad in the region,
Sixteen and strong as a man—was a man, by God!—
And the double-bit bit into red oak, and in that rhythm,
In his head, all day, marched the Greek paradigm:
That was all that was his, and all he could carry all day with him.

Λέγω, λέγεις, λέγει, and the axe swung.
That was that year, and the next year we see him
Revolve in his dream between the piece goods and cheese,
In a crossroads store, between peppermint candy and plow-points,
While the eaves drip, and beyond the black trees of winter
Last light grays out, and in the ruts of the lane
Water gleams, sober as steel. That was that land,
And that was the life, and he reached out and
Took the dime from the gray-scaled palm of the Negro plowhand's hand.

'Εν ἀρχῇ ἦν ὁ λόγος: in the beginning
Was the word, but in the end was
What? At the mirror, lather on chin, with a razor

Big as a corn-knife, or, so to the boy it seemed,
He stood, and said: 'Eν ἀρχῇ ἦν ὁ λόγος:
And laughed. And said: "That's Greek, now you know how it sounds!"
And laughed, and waved the bright blade like a toy.
And laughing from the deep of a dark conquest and joy,
Said: "Greek—but it wasn't for me. Let's get to breakfast, boy."

## 3 FOX-FIRE: 1956

Years later, I find the old grammar, yellowed. Night
Is falling. Ash flakes from the log. The log
Glows, winks, wanes. Westward, the sky,
In one small area redeemed from gray, bleeds dully.
Beyond my window, athwart that red west,
The spruce bough, though snow-burdened, looks black,
Not white. The world lives by the trick of the eye, the trick
Of the heart. I hold the book in my hand, but God
—In what mercy, if mercy?—will not let me weep. But I
Do not want to weep. I want to understand.

Oh, let me understand what is that sound,
Like wind, that fills the enormous dark of my head.
Beyond my head there is no wind, the room
Darkening, the world beyond the room darkening,
And no wind beyond to cleave, unclot, the thickening
Darkness. There must be a way to state the problem.
The statement of a problem, no doubt, determines solution.
If once, clear and distinct, I could state it, then God
Could no longer fall back on His old alibi of ignorance.
I hear now my small son laugh from a farther room.

I know he sits there and laughs among his toys,
Teddy bear, letter blocks, yellow dumptruck, derrick, choo-choo—
Bright images, all, of Life's significance.
So I put the book on the shelf, beside my own grammar,
Unopened these thirty years, and leave the dark room,
And know that all night, while the constellations grind,
Beings with folded wings brood above that shelf,
Awe-struck and imbecile, and in the dark,
Amid History's vice and velleity, that poor book burns
Like fox-fire in the black swamp of the world's error.

## 4 IN THE TURPITUDE OF TIME: N. D.

In the turpitude of Time,
Hope dances on the razor edge.
I see those ever healing feet
Tread the honed edge above despair.
I see the song-wet lip and tossing hair.

The leaf unfolds the autumn weather.
The heart spills the horizon's light.
In the woods, the hunter, weeping, kneels,
And the dappled fawn weeps in contrition
For its own beauty. I hear the toad's intercession

For us, and all, who do not know
How cause flows backward from effect
To bless the past occasion, and
How Time's tongue lifts only to tell,
Minute by minute, what truth the brave heart will fulfill.

Can we—oh, could we only—believe
What annelid and osprey know,
And the stone, night-long, groans to divulge?
If we could only, then that star
That dawnward slants might sing to our human ear,

And joy, in daylight, run like feet,
And strength, in darkness, wait like hands,
And between the stone and the wind's voice
A silence wait to become our own song:
In the heart's last kingdom only the old are young.

## 5 A VISION: CIRCA 1880

Out of the woods where pollen is a powder of gold
Shaken from pistil of oak minutely, and of maple,
And is falling, and the tulip tree lifts, not yet tarnished,
The last calyx, in which chartreuse coolness recessed, dew,
Only this morning, lingered till noon—look,
Out of the woods, barefoot, the boy comes. He stands,
Hieratic, complete, in patched britches and that idleness of boyhood
Which asks nothing and is its own fulfilment:
In his hand a wand of peeled willow, boy-idle and aimless.

Poised between woods and the pasture, sun-green and green shadow,
Hair sweat-dark, brow bearing a smudge of gold pollen, lips
Parted in some near-smile of boyhood bemusement,
Dangling the willow, he stands, and I—I stare
Down the tube and darkening corridor of Time
That breaks, like tears, upon that sunlit space,
And staring, I know who he is, and would cry out.
Out of my knowledge, I would cry out and say:
*Listen!* Say: *Listen! I know—oh, I know—let me tell you!*

That scene is in Trigg County, and I see it.
Trigg County is in Kentucky, and I have been there,
But never remember the spring there. I remember

A land of cedar-shade, blue, and the purl of limewater,
But the pasture parched, and the voice of the lost joree
Unrelenting as conscience, and sick, and the afternoon throbs,
And the sun's hot eye on the dry leaf shrivels the aphid,
And the sun's heel does violence in the corn-balk.
That is what I remember, and so the scene

I had seen just now in the mind's eye, vernal,
Is altered, and I strive to cry across the dry pasture,
But cannot, nor move, for my feet, like dry corn-roots, cleave
Into the hard earth, and my tongue makes only the dry,
Slight sound of wind on the autumn corn-blade. The boy,
With imperial calm, crosses a space, rejoins
The shadow of woods, but pauses, turns, grins once,
And is gone. And one high oak leaf stirs gray, and the air,
Stirring, freshens to the far favor of rain.

## *Fatal Interview: Penthesilea and Achilles*

Beautiful, bold, shaking the gold glint of sun-foil,
Which light is, scurrying, scouring the plain now, she rides
To distribute man-death, Greek-death—oh, she is the darling
Of war, Troy, and Ares, her black-bristled father, whose toil
Was her dream on the moonlit pillow. She moaned in that dream of blood-moil.

She never remembered her dream at advent of daylight,
But sat with breasts heavy, eyes sad, and the honey tasteless,
And her only pleasure for morning to finger the sword edge
Till from lucky unstitching on thumb-ball one drop blushed to sight;
Then with blood sweet on tongue, she watched bees weave, sun-glinting,
and dreamed of night.

Look, look—Greeks flee! For who can withstand Beauty's rage?
Her arrows are spilling afar what will unparch earth now.
Leaping in knee-clip, her courser neighs loud and rolls red eye,
But her heart is yet latched, for only one death can assauge
That heart's deepest need. Yes, let him come forth to her dire tutelage.

From shameful grief, sloth, vanity, and mere pique,
He lifts forth now, spits in his palm for the spear-haft,
Hawks up his phlegm, looms in his darkening selfhood:
Fame-fed, blood-fat as a tick, Ambition's geek.
She leaps from horse, hurls spear; hears laughter, then, from the Greek.

Her mount—how well trained!—waits. She waits, ungirt—
Or at least she has felt so since first the spear flew from handgrip;
And worse, as that Greek grins. He grins. He waits. Will he say:
"Fool girl, get home to your dolls—darn socks, mend a shirt!"
Oh, she couldn't bear that! She'd die, rather. But wonders how much it would hurt.

Where lungs divide to hang belly, the spear-flight first pricks her;
Under breastplate slides weightily in; in blood-darkness shears backbone;
Emerges in sunlight, though briefly; finds the mount waiting, faithful,
And with the same force unallayed it had used to transfix her,
Transfixes the brute, knocks it down; and thus on that pincushion sticks her.

How slow the whole process seemed to the hero who watched it,
Who had dreamed it a thousand times, though without recognition.
How sad all the past years of fame, as he tore off her breastplate
And saw the first globèd sweet handful, then the other that matched it.
His life went like dust on his tongue; he wept, for he knew he had botched it.

"Aie!" he cried out, "I have lolled in a thousand laps,
I have cracked heads by thousands, spilled buckets of blood, like water,
But woe is my soul that it's this sweet blood I spill now,
For this is my True Love—oh, darling, except for mishaps,
You had lain on a bed far softer than this while I mammocked those paps!"

"Aie!" cried Thersites, the foul-mouth, "so it's *aie,* you snot!
What odds, what odds, you splash like a brat in his bathtub.
Oh, you'd kill all the men, debauch all the boys, tup the women,
And if one escapes, you start sniveling—" But further saith not,
For hand of the hero breaks jawbone, and brain-pan is dumped on the spot:

Past areas of combat and cultivation, like thunder,
Now History, on the far hill-line, gathers. The hero's great spear-head
Withdraws, and flesh-suction sighs sad, once. The hero waits, rapt,
In blue sun-blaze, on sea-plain. One crow beats up past Scamander,
And will pluck the blue eyes that, puzzled, stare up at blue sky they lie under.

## *Some Quiet, Plain Poems*

### 1 ORNITHOLOGY IN A WORLD OF FLUX

It was only a bird call at evening, unidentified,
As I came from the spring with water, across the rocky back-pasture;
But so still I stood sky above was not stiller than sky in pail-water.

Years pass, all places and faces fade, some people have died,
And I stand in a far land, the evening still, and am at last sure
That I miss more that stillness at bird-call than some things that were to fail later.

## 2 HOLLY AND HICKORY

Rain, all night, taps the holly.
It ticks like a telegraph on the pane.
If awake in that house, meditating some old folly
Or trying to live an old pleasure again,
I could hear it sluicing the ruts in the lane.

Rain beats down the last leaf of hickory,
But where I lie now rain sounds hint less
At benign sleight of the seasons, or Time's adept trickery,
And with years I feel less joy or distress
To hear water moving in wheel ruts, star-glintless,

And if any car comes now up that lane,
It carries nobody I could know,
And who wakes in that house now to hear the rain
May fall back to sleep—as I, long ago,
Who dreamed dawnward; and would rise to go.

## 3 THE WELL HOUSE

What happened there, it was not much,
But was enough. If you come back,
*Not much* may be *too much,* even if you have your old knack
Of stillness, and do not touch
A thing, a broken toy or rusted tool or any such
Object you happen to find
Hidden where, uncontrolled, grass and weeds bend.

The clematis that latches the door
Of the ruinous well house, you might break it.
Though guessing the water foul now, and not thirsting to take it,
With thirst from those years before
You might lean over the coping to stare at the water's dark-glinting floor.
Yes, that might be the event
To change *not much* to *too much,* and more than meant.

Yes, Truth is always in balance, and
*Not much* can become *too much* so quick.
Suppose you came back and found your heart suddenly sick,
And covered your sight with your hand:
Your tears might mean more than the thing you wept for but did not understand.
Yes, something might happen there
If you came back—even if you just stood to stare.

## 4 IN MOONLIGHT, SOMEWHERE, THEY ARE SINGING

Under the maples at moonrise—
Moon whitening top leaf of the white oak
That rose from the dark mass of maples and range of eyes—
They were singing together, and I woke

From my sleep to the whiteness of moon-fire,
And deep from their dark maples, I
Could hear the two voices shake silver and free, and aspire
To be lost in moon-vastness of the sky.

My young aunt and her young husband
From their dark maples sang, and though
Too young to know what they meant I was happy and
So slept, for I knew I would come to know.

But what of the old man awake there,
As the voices, like vine, climbed up moonlight?
What thought did he think of past time as they twined bright in moon-air,
And veined, with their silver, the moon-flesh of night?

Far off, I recall, in the barn lot,
A mule stamped, once; but the song then
Was over, and for that night, or forever, would not
Resume—but should it again,

Years after, wake me to white moon-fire
On pillow, high oak leaf, and far field,
I should hope to find imaged in what new voices aspire
Some life-faith yet, by my years, unrepealed.

## 5 IN ITALIAN THEY CALL THE BIRD *CIVETTA*

The evening drooped toward owl-call,
The small moon slid pale down the sky,
Dark was decisive in cedars,
But dust down the lane dreamed pale,
And my feet stirred that dust there—
Ah, I see that Kentucky scene
Now only behind my shut eyelids,
As in this far land I stand
At the selfsame ambiguous hour
In the heart's ambiguity,
And Time is crumpled like paper
Crushed in my hand, while here
*The thin moon slants pale down the pale sky,*
*And the small owl mourns from the moat.*

This small owl calls from the moat now.
That other owl answers him
Across all the years and miles that
Are the only Truth I have learned,
And back from the present owl-call
Burns backward the blaze of day,
And the passage of years, like a tire's scream,
Fades now while the reply

Of a dew-damp and downy lost throat spills
To quaver from that home-dark,
And frame between owl-call and owl-call,
Life's bright parenthesis.

*The thin moon slants pale down the pale sky:*
*The small owl mourns from the moat.*

## 6 DEBATE: QUESTION, QUARRY, DREAM

*Asking what, asking what?*—all a boy's afternoon,
Squatting in the canebrake where the muskrat will come.
*Muskrat, muskrat, please now, please, come soon.*
He comes, stares, goes, lets the question resume.
He has taken whatever answer may be down to his mud-burrow gloom.

*Seeking what, seeking what?*—foot soft in cedar-shade.
Was that a deer-flag white past windfall and fern?
No, but by bluffside lurk powers and in the fern-glade
Tall presences, standing all night, like white fox-fire burn.
The small fox lays his head in your hand now and weeps that you go, not to return.

*Dreaming what, dreaming what?*—lying on the hill at twilight,
Still air stirred only by moth wing, and last stain of sun
Fading to moth-sky, blood-red to moth-white and starlight,
And Time leans down to kiss the heart's ambition,
While far away, before moonrise, come the town lights, one by one.

Long since that time I have walked night streets, heel-iron
Clicking the stone, and in dark in windows have stared.
Question, quarry, dream—I have vented my ire on
My own heart that, ignorant and untoward,
Yearns for an absolute that Time would, I thought, have prepared,

But has not yet. Well, let us debate
The issue. But under a tight roof, clutching a toy,
My son now sleeps, and when the hour grows late,
I shall go forth where the cold constellations deploy
And lift up my eyes to consider more strictly the appalling logic of joy.

## *Ballad: Between the Boxcars (1923)*

### 1 I CAN'T EVEN REMEMBER THE NAME

I can't even remember the name of the one who fell
Flat on his ass, on the cinders, between the boxcars.
I can't even remember whether he got off his yell
Before what happened had happened between the boxcars.

But whether or not he managed to get off his yell,
I remember its shape on his mouth, between the boxcars,
And it was shape that yours would be too if you fell
Flat on your ass, on the cinders, between the boxcars.

And one more thing I remember perfectly well,
You go for the grip at the front, not the back, of the boxcars.
Miss the front, you're knocked off—miss the back, you never can tell
But you're flat on your ass, on the cinders, between the boxcars.

He was fifteen and old enough to know perfectly well
You try for the grip at the front, not the back, of the boxcars,
But he was the kind of smart aleck you always can tell
Ends flat on his ass, on the cinders, between the boxcars.

Suppose I remembered his name, then what the hell
Good would it do him now between the boxcars?
But it might mean something to me if I could tell
You the name of the one who fell between the boxcars.

## 2 HE WAS FORMIDABLE

He was formidable, he was, the little booger,
As he spat in his hands and picked up the Louisville Slugger,
And at that bat-crack
Around those bases he could sure ball the jack,
And if from the outfield the peg had beat him home,
He would slide in slick, like a knife in a nigger.
So we dreamed of an afternoon to come,
In the Series, the ninth-inning hush, in the Yankee Stadium,
Sun low, score tied, bases full, two out, and he'd waltz to the plate with his grin—
But no, oh no, not now, not ever! for in
That umpireless rhubarb and brute-heeled hugger-mugger,
He got spiked sliding home, got spiked between the boxcars.

Oh, his hair was brown-bright as a chestnut, sun-glinting and curly,
And that lip that smiled boy-sweet could go, of a sudden, man-surly,
And the way he was built
Made the girls in his grade in dark stare, and finger the quilt.
Yes, he was the kind you know born to give many delight,
And entering on such life-labor early,
Would have moved, bemused, in that rhythm and rite,
Through blood-throbbing blackness and moon-gleam
and pearly thigh-glimmer of night,
To the exquisite glut: *Woman Slays Self for His Love,* as the tabloids would tell—
But no, never now! Like a kid in his first brothel,

In that hot clasp and loveless hurly-burly,
    He spilled, as boys may, too soon, between the boxcars.

Oh, he might have been boss of the best supermarket in town,
Bright with banners and chrome, where housewives push carts up and down,
And morning and night
Walked the street with his credit *A*-rated and blood pressure right,
His boy a dentist in Nashville, his girl at State Normal;
Or a scientist flushed with *Time*-cover renown
For vaccine, or bomb, or smog removal;
Or a hero with phiz like hewn cedar, though young for the stars of a general,
Descending the steps of his personal plane to view the home-town unveiling.
But no, never now!—battle-cunning, the test tube, retailing,
All, all, in a helter-skeltering mishmash thrown
    To that clobber and grind, too soon, between the boxcars.

But what is success, or failure, at the last?
The newspaper whirled down the track when the through freight has passed
Will sink from that gust
To be of such value as it intrinsically must,
And why should we grieve for the name that boy might have made
To be printed on newsprint like that, for that blast
To whirl with the wheels' fanfaronade,
When we cannot even remember his name, nor humbly have prayed
That when that blunt grossness, slam-banging, bang-slamming, blots black
the last blue flash of sky,
And our own lips utter the crazed organism's cry,
We may know the poor self not alone, but with all who are cast
    To that clobber and slobber and grunt, between the boxcars?

## 3 HE HAS FLED

He has fled like electricity down the telegraph wires into
prairies of distance where the single bird
sits small and black against the saffron sky,
and is itself.

He has fled like the glint of glory down the April-wet
rails, toward sunset.

He has fled like the wild goose, north-beaked and star-treading,
with night-hoot too high to be heard by whoever
stands now to brood where the last, lost spur of
the Canadian Pacific ends.

He has retired into the cold chemical combustion where water
at last probes the fibers of the creosote-treated
crosstie.

He has retired where the acrid sap of red oak rises under the
iron bark, and he does not now scream at
the saw-bite.

He has retired into the delectable crystallization of sugar
in grape jelly stored twenty years in a cellar,
in a Burgundian drowse.

He has propounded a theorem the refutation of which would devalue
all our anguish.

He has broken past atmospheres, and the lungs breathe rarefaction
of revelation and the head now reels,
like Truth.

He has explored a calculus of your unexpected probabilities,
and what now *is* was never probable,
but only *is*,

For we are in the world and nothing is good enough, which is
to say that the world is here and we are not
good enough,

And we live in the world, and in so far as we live, the world
continues to live in us,

Despite all we can do to reject it utterly, including
this particular recollection, which now I
would eject, reject,
but cannot.

## *Two Studies in Idealism: Short Survey of American, and Human, History*

*For Allan Nevins*

### 1 BEAR TRACK PLANTATION: SHORTLY AFTER SHILOH

Two things a man's built for, killing and you-know-what.
As for you-know-what, I reckon I taken my share,
Bed-ease or bush-whack, but killing—hell, three's all I got,
And he promised me ten, Jeff Davis, the bastard. 'Taint fair.

'Taint fair, a man rides and knows he won't live forever,
And a man needs something to take with him when he dies.
Ain't much worth taking, but what happens under the cover
Or at the steel-point—yeah, that look in their eyes.

That same look, it comes in their eyes when you give 'em the business.
It's something a man can hang on to, come black-frost or sun.
Come hell or high water, it's something to save from the mess,
No matter whatever else you never got done.

For a second it seems like a man can know what he lives for,
When those eyelids go waggle, or maybe the eyes pop wide,
And that look comes there. Yeah, Christ, then you know who you are—
And will maybe remember that much even after you've died.

But now I lie worrying what look my own eyes got
When that Blue-Belly caught me off balance. Did that look mean then
That I'd honed for something not killing or you-know-what?
Hell, no. I'd lie easy if Jeff had just give me that ten.

## 2 HARVARD '61: BATTLE FATIGUE

I didn't mind dying—it wasn't that at all.
It behooves a man to prove manhood by dying for Right.
If you die for Right that fact is your dearest requital,
But you find it disturbing when others die who simply haven't the right.

Why should they die with that obscene insouciance?
They seem to insult the principle of your own death.
Touch pitch, be defiled: it was hard to keep proper distance
From such unprincipled wastrels of blood and profligates of breath.

I tried to slay without rancor, and often succeeded.
I tried to keep the heart pure, though hand took stain.
But they made it so hard for me, the way they proceeded
To parody with their own dying that Death which only Right should sustain.

Time passed. It got worse. It seemed like a plot against me.
I said they had made their own evil bed and lay on it,
But they grinned in the dark—they grinned—and I yet see
That last one. At woods-edge we held, and over the stubble they came with bayonet.

He uttered his yell, he was there!—teeth yellow, some missing.
*Why, he's old as my father,* I thought, finger frozen on trigger.
I saw the ambeer on his whiskers, heard the old breath hissing.
The puncture came small on his chest. 'Twas nothing. The stain then got bigger.

And he said: "Why, son, you done done it—I figgered I'd skeered ye."
Said: "Son, you look puke-pale. Buck up! If it hadn't been you,
Some other young squirt would a-done it." I stood, and weirdly
The tumult of battle went soundless, like gesture in dream. And I was dead, too.

Dead, and had died for the Right, as I had a right to,
And glad to be dead, and hold my residence
Beyond life's awful illogic, and the world's stew,
Where people who haven't the right just die, with ghastly impertinence.

## *Nocturne: Traveling Salesman in Hotel Bedroom*

The toothbrush lies in its case,
    Like you in your coffin when
The mourners come to stare
    And the bristles grow on your chin.

Oh, the soap lies in the dish,
    Dissolving from every pore,
Like your poor heart in the breast
    When the clock strikes once, and once more.

The toilet gurgles and whines,
    Like History absorbing event,
For process is all, and who cares
    What any particular has meant?

Far off, in the predawn drizzle,
    A car's tires slosh the street mess,
And you think, in an access of anguish,
    It bears someone to happiness,

Or at least to a destination
    Where duty is clear, and sleep deep,
And the image of self, in dark standing,
    Does not pluck at the hangnail, and weep,

But you're practical, and know
    That wherever that place lies
You would find few customers there
    For your line of merchandise,

And there's nothing, in fact, really wrong here:
    Take a slug of Old Jack neat,
Try a chapter in the Gideon,
    Then work on the sales sheet,

And vision is possible, and
    Man's meed of glory not
Impossible—oh remember,
    Remember—in life's upshot.

## *So You Agree with What I Say? Well, What Did I Say?*

Albino-pale, half-blind, his orbit revolved
Between his Bible and the cobbler's bench,
With all human complexities resolved
In that Hope past deprivation, or any heart-wrench.

Or so it seemed—and at dusk we'd see him head back
To his place with a can of pork and beans, and some bread,
And once, when he'd lighted his lamp, we spied in the shack
To see him eat beans, then over his book bend his head.

In the summer dusk we would see him heading home,
Past the field where after supper we played baseball
Till the grass got dew-slick and a grounder out of the gloom
Might knock out your teeth, and our mothers began to call.

Past Old Man Duckett out fixing that hinge on his gate,
Past all the Cobb family admiring their new Chevrolet,
Past the moonvines that hid Sue Cramm in the swing with her date,
Whose hand was already up under her dress, halfway—

He would move past us all. And the bat cracked, and the fly
Popped up from our shadow to spin in the high, last light.
Like a little world, the ball hung there spinning, high,
With the side to the setting sun glimmering white.

Mr. Moody is dead long back, and some of the boys
Who played in that ball game dead too, by disease or violence,
But others went on to their proper successes, and joys,
And made contribution to social and scientific improvements,

And with those improvements, I now am ready to say
That if God short-changed Mr. Moody, it's time for Him
To give up this godding business, and make way
For somebody else to try, or an IBM.

## *Prognosis: A Short Story, the End of Which You Will Know Soon Enough*

1 AND OH—

She was into her forties, her daughter slick, sly, and no good;
The son-in-law sweet, booze-bit, much given to talk at twilight,
After tea was removed and drink brought, for he said she alone understood;
And her husband withdrawn in his gloom of success.
Yes, that was her family, she loved them, yes,
But now sat and continued to stare
At the strong hand, white-scrubbed, sprigged with black recalcitrant hair,
And what the voice said she couldn't imagine, or guess,
For the hairs were so black, and a wind to blow
Was gathered below some horizon, and the hairs were so black, and oh,

It was cancer, and oh, felt her face smiling stiff like dried mud,
And went out, felt her thighs as they moved in the street, oh white, and oh,
Moving white in their dark, under silk, under fur, and the multitude
Trod past in their fleshy agitation,
And sun sank, and oh, the flesh clung to bone,
"And, daughter, and oh—" she then tried,
But the daughter said, "Later, I'm doing my hair," and the mother replied,
"So you went to a hotel today with someone,"
And the daughter said sweetly, "But how did you know?"
Said, "Look, how he bruised me—and don't you wish it was you?" And oh,

She wished it, she wished it, and felt her face flaming for shame,
For she knew no word had been uttered, the words only words in her head,

And the daughter's hair, gold, spilled like light, till an anguish without name
Stark shook her. She fled and in twilight found
The son-in-law sitting, first drink not yet downed,
And by fireside said, "Listen—for I—"
But the guests had arrived, they smiled, and the Beast, like a kitten gone shy,
Crept under a chair and from shadow stared forth with no sound,
And the dinner was lovely, they all said so,
And she suddenly saw how all faces were beautiful, hearts pure, and oh,

She loved them, she did, as they glimmered through tears, and wine whirled,
So threw her head back, like a girl laughed for joy, husband watching, and oh,
In dark later his hand was laid on her—in dark, as when, oh, ungirled—
And she shook, she said, "No," but he made headway.
"But the doctor—the doctor—" she tried to say,
Then said it, and oh, she knew she would die,
But he, in that stubborn occupation, made no reply,
For as though provoked at her words, there was sudden essay
Of old force that she long had thought spent, but no,
By blunt bruteness, in love or in hate, she was racked, she was rent, and oh,

Time was not Time now—and once as a child she had lain
On the grass, in spring dusk, under maples, to watch the first fireflies,
So prayed now, "God, please—" but *please what* didn't know, so slept, woke again,
And with eyes wide in dark simply stared in the dark there,
One finger yet tangled in his sparse chest-hair,
Which for years, as she knew, had been gray,
And was pitiful of that sad stranger who had come his own difficult way,
And at last, with her anguish exhausted, and past despair,
Dreamed a field of white lilies wind-shimmering, slow,
And wept, wept for joy, beneath the dark glory of the world's name, and oh—

*And oh.*

## 2 WHAT THE SAND SAID

—and God, God, somewhere, *she said,* are lilies, in a field, white,
and let me guess where, where they are, but I don't know, and a slight
wind moves them slow, *and she lay shuddering and white under the dark glory of*
*whatever is the world's name,* and oh—
what must I dream of, what—*and said,*
if I dream, I shall be real, or really
myself, and oh,
if I am myself, let me lie shuddering and white, please, under the
dark glory of the world's name, and oh—
or at least, not being myself, let whatever
glint in dark my dream is, glimmer like ice,
like steel, like the wickedest
star, please, but let my dream be, being whatever it needs to be in order
to be what it is,
for, dear God, I love
it, and love the world, and I do not grieve to be lost in whatever
awfulness of dark the
world may be, and love is, and oh—
and dawn and dark are the glory we know,
and oh—

I have heard the grain of sand say: I know my joy, I know its name.

## 3 WHAT THE JOREE SAID, THE JOREE BEING ONLY A BIRD

The joree sang. What does he sing? He says
*Joree.* But *joree,* what does *joree* mean? It means
Joree, for he sings his sweet sadness of self, and the ways
Of the singing say only himself where the cedar leans
Black on white limestone, oh, listen! Lost in the day-blaze,
Foot set on white stone, stone hot through leather, she came
Down the path, she a girl, and the enormity of sun-blaze consumed her name.

*Who was I? Who was I? Oh, tell me my name!* But the bird
Only sang, said *joree,* and so she came where the spring
Flowed out from the stone, silver-braiding, brim-swelling, and stirred
The chlorophyll green of pale cress leaf submerged there. So sing,
Say *joree,* for her wrist, lax in water, trailed white, and oh, see,
How sun through closed eyelids is blood and red blood-throb. The bird said *joree,*

And in fullness of Time she would say: *All truth comes unwitting,*
*For I set heel on worm-head, and relished dawn-stool more than sunrise.*
*I spat on my shadow in sunlight, and at the sun's setting*
*Clasped hands on belly. But stared in the dentist's pale eyes*
*And yearned for the drill-stab, for yes, I loved God, though forgetting*
*His name.* But remembered the joree, so wished she might utter
Herself in that sweet, sad asseverant candor, from black shade,
in day-blaze, by water.

## *Autumnal Equinox on Mediterranean Beach*

Sail-bellyer, exciter of boys, come bang
To smithereens doors, and see if I give a hang,

For I am sick of summer and the insane glitter
Of sea sun-bit, and the wavelets that bicker and titter,

And the fat girls that hang out brown breasts like fruit overripe,
And the thin ones flung pale in rock-shadow, goose-pimpled as tripe,

And the young men who pose on the headlands like ads for Jantzen,
And the old who would do so much better to keep proper pants on,

And all Latin faeces one finds, like jewels, in the sand,
And the gaze of the small, sweet octopus fondling your hand.

Come howl like a prophet the season's righteous anger,
And knock down our idols with crash, bang, or clangor.

Blow the cat's fur furry sideways, make dogs bark,
Blow the hen's tail feathers forward past the pink mark,

Snatch the laundry off the line, like youth away,
Blow plastered hair off the bald spot, lift toupee.

Come blow old women's skirts, bring Truth to light,
Though at such age morn's all the same as night.

Come swirl old picnic papers to very sky-height,
And make gulls gabble in fury at such breach of their air-right.

Kick up the bay now, make a mess of it,
Fling spume in our sinful faces, like God's spit,

For now all our pleasures, like peaches, get rotten, not riper,
And summer is over, and time to pay the piper,

And be glad to do it, for man's not made for much pleasure,
Or even for joy, unless cut down to his measure.

Yes, kick the garbage pail, and scatter garbage,
That the cat flee forth with fish-head, the housewife rage,

For pain and pleasure balance in God's year—
Though *whose* is *which* is not your problem here,

And perhaps not even God's. So bang, wind, batter,
While human hearts do the bookkeeping in this matter.

## *Nursery Rhymes*

### 1 KNOCKETY-KNOCKETY-KNOCK

Hickory-dickory-dock—
The mouse ran up the clock.
The clock struck one,
And I fell down,
Hickory-dickory-dock.
God let me fall down,
And I tore my nightgown,
And knockety-knockety-knock,
As I lie on the floor,
Someone's at the door—
Hickory-dickory-dock.

Hickory-dickory-dock—
The mouse runs up the clock.
My father took me
For a ride on his knee,
Hickory-dickory-dock.
But then things were nice,
With no awful mice,
And no knockety-knockety-knock,
And my head didn't spin
When the strange foot came in—
Hickory-dickory-dock.

Hickory-dickory-dock—
The mouse runs up the clock.
When I'd wake in the night,
Mother held me tight,
Hickory-dickory-dock.
Then dreams were just dreams,
And not, as it now seems,
A knockety-knockety-knock
That walks in at the door
As I lie on the floor—
Hickory-dickory-dock.

Hickory-dickory-dock—
The mouse ran up the clock,
And the clock struck one
And my poor head spun,
Hickory-dickory-dock,
And Ma's deader than mackerel,
And Pa pickled as pickerel,
And oh! knockety-knockety-knock,
God's red eyes glare
From sockets of dark air—
Knockety-knockety-knock.

## 2 NEWS OF UNEXPECTED DEMISE OF LITTLE BOY BLUE

Little Boy Blue, come blow your horn,
The sheep's in the meadow, the cow's in the corn.
Little Boy, will you make me stand and call
From first dawn-robin to last dew-fall?
It's no excuse you are young and careless,
With your thing-a-bob little and your little chest hairless,
For people have duties to perform at all ages—
Hurry up, Little Boy, or I'll dock your wages.

Come blow your horn, Little Boy Blue,
Or I'll make your bottom the bluest part of you.
Come blow your horn, you Little Gold-bricker,
Or I'll snatch you baldheaded in a wink, or quicker.
Little Boy, you'll get no more ice cream.
Nobody will come when you have a bad dream.
Where is that pretty little horn I gave you?
I simply won't tolerate such behavior.

I should have known you'd be derelict.
From a family like yours what can we expect?
Born of woman, and she grunted like a pig,
Got by man just for the frig,

Dropped in the world like a package of offal,
Demanding love with wail and snuffle,
Lost in the world and the trees were tall—
You Little Wretch, don't you hear me call!

A plague and a pox on such a bad boy.
I know you are hiding just to annoy.
You reflect no credit on the human race.
You stand in need of prayer and grace.
Where's that Little Wretch that tends the sheep?

*He's under the haystack, fast asleep.*

Well, damn it, go wake him!

*No, not I—*

*I can only walk the green fields, and cry.*

## 3 MOTHER MAKES THE BISCUITS

Mother makes the biscuits,
Father makes the laws,
Grandma wets the bed sometimes,
Kitty-cats have claws.

Mother sweeps the kitchen,
Father milks the cow,
Grandpa leaves his pants unbuttoned,
Puppy-dogs bark, *bow-wow.*

All do as God intends,
The sun sets in the west,
Father shaves his chin, *scrape-scrape,*
Mother knows best.

Clap hands, children,
Clap hands and sing!
Hold hands together, children,
And dance in a ring,

For the green worm sings on the leaf,
The black beetle folds hands to pray,
And the stones in the field wash their faces clean
To meet break of day.

But we may see this only
Because all night we have stared
At the black miles past where stars are
Till the stars disappeared.

## 4 THE BRAMBLE BUSH

There was a man in our town
And he was wondrous wise,
He jumped into a bramble bush
And scratched out both his eyes,

And could not see the pretty sky,
Or how, whenever you throw
A stone into a sparrow-tree,
All wheel like one, and go.

So when he saw he could not see,
And knew the fact was plain,
He jumped back into the bramble bush
And scratched them in again,

And I now saw past the fartherest stars
How darkness blazed like light,
And the sun was a winking spark that rose
Up the chimney of the night,

And like petals from a wind-torn bough
In furious beauty blown,
The stars were gone—and I heard the joy
Of flesh singing on the bone.

## *Short Thoughts for Long Nights*

### 1 NIGHTMARE OF MOUSE

It was there, but I said it couldn't be true in daylight.
It was there, but I said it was only a trick of starlight.
It was there, but I said to believe it would take a fool,
And I wasn't, so didn't—till teeth crunched on my skull.

## 2 NIGHTMARE OF MAN

I assembled, marshaled, my data, deployed them expertly.
My induction was perfect, as far as induction may be.
But the formula failed in the test tube, despite all my skill,
For I'd thought of the death of my mother, and wept; and weep still.

## 3 COLLOQUY WITH COCKROACH

I know I smell. But everyone does, somewhat.
I smell this way only because I crawl down the drain.
I've no slightest idea how you got the smell you've got.
No, I haven't time now—it might take you too long to explain.

## 4 LITTLE BOY ON VOYAGE

Little boy, little boy, standing on ship-shudder, wide eyes staring
At unease of ocean, at sunset, and the distance long—
You've stared, little boy, at gray distance past hoping or despairing,
So come in for supper and sleep, now; they, too, will help you grow strong.

## 5 OBSESSION

Dawn draws on slow when dawn brings only dawn:
Only slow milk-wash on window, star paling, first bird-stir,
Sweat cold now on pillow, before the alarm's *burr*,
And the old thought for the new day as day draws on.

## 6 JOY

If you've never had it, discussion is perfectly fruitless,
And if you have, you can tell nobody about it.
To explain silence, you scarcely try to shout it.
Let the flute and drum be still, the trumpet *toot*less.

## 7 CRICKET, ON KITCHEN FLOOR, ENTERS HISTORY

History, shaped like white hen,
Walked in at kitchen door.
Beak clicked once on stone floor.
Out door walked hen then;
But will, no doubt, come again.

## 8 LITTLE BOY AND GENERAL PRINCIPLE

Don't cry, little boy, you see it is only natural
That little red trucks will break, whether plastic or tin,
And some other things, too. It's a general principle
That you'll have to learn soon, so you might, I guess, begin.

## 9 GRASSHOPPER TRIES TO BREAK SOLIPSISM

Sing *summer, summer,* sing *summer* summerlong—
For God is light, oh I love Him, love is my song.
I sing, for I must, for God, if I didn't, would weep,
And over all things, all night, His despair, like ice, creep.

## *About the Author*

ROBERT PENN WARREN was born in Guthrie, Kentucky, in 1905. He entered Vanderbilt University at the age of sixteen and graduated *summa cum laude;* he went to the University of California for his master's degree, then to Yale University, and in 1928 to Oxford as a Rhodes Scholar.

Mr. Warren began his teaching career at Southwestern College (1930-31) and Vanderbilt University (1931-34). He moved to Louisiana State University in 1934, and was one of the founders and editors of *The Southern Review.* From 1942 to 1950 he was Professor of English at the University of Minnesota (and Consultant in Poetry at the Library of Congress, 1944-45). From 1951 to 1956 he was a member of the faculty of Yale University.

In 1939 Mr. Warren published his first novel, *Night Rider* (reissued by Random House in 1948) and won his first Guggenheim Fellowship. In 1943 came *At Heaven's Gate,* and in 1946, *All the King's Men* (Pulitzer Prize). These were followed by *World Enough and Time* (1950) *Band of Angels* (1955) and *The Cave* (1959). Mr. Warren has also published a short-story collection, *The Circus in the Attic,* in addition to many textbooks and critical studies (*Selected Essays* appeared in 1958).

In 1935, his first collection of lyrics, *Thirty-six Poems,* appeared. *Eleven Poems on the Same Theme* (1942) won the Shelley Memorial Award, followed in 1944 by *Selected Poems. Brother to Dragons: A Tale in Verse and Voices* appeared in 1953, and *Promises: Poems 1954-1956* in 1957 (Pulitzer Prize, National Book Award).

Mr. Warren lives in Connecticut with his wife, Eleanor Clark, whose most recent book is *Rome and a Villa,* and their two children, Rosanna and Gabriel.